The Chimney Sweep

It was still dark when Jake woke up. Mr
shaking Jake's shoulder. 'Come on, get up, you lazy
little urchin. There are lots of chimneys to sweep,'
he grumbled.

Jake tried to rub the sleep from his eyes. He was
tired, cold, and hungry. He tied his woollen scarf
more tightly round his neck and buttoned up his
ragged jacket. He didn't have any socks so he pushed
his bare feet into his old boots. His fingers were
cold and it was hard work tying the strings that
he had to use instead of laces.

1

Even though he was very hungry Jake could not
eat the piece of hard cheese that Mr Webster had
put out for his breakfast. He dropped it under the
table for Scruff, Mr Webster's dog. Scruff wagged his
tail and licked Jake's hand.

'Did you see that, Mr Webster?' said Slim, his
helper. 'That boy doesn't seem to be enjoying his food.
He's given it to that scruffy dog again.'

'Has he?' snarled Mr Webster. 'Well, if he doesn't
like the food I give him, he'll have to go hungry.'

When Mr Webster had finished his breakfast he went to the cupboard and pulled out his chimney-sweeping brushes. 'Carry those,' he snapped, throwing them in a heap at Jake's feet. 'It's a long way to the Manor House and it's time we got going. We have twenty chimneys to sweep today.'

Jake picked up the heavy bundle of brushes and followed Mr Webster and his assistant out into the crisp morning air.

Mr Webster and Slim rode on the painted cart and
Jake ran behind them with the brushes. The wheels
of the cart clattered over the cobble stones leaving
tracks in the newly fallen snow. Jake slipped and
slid as he tried to keep his balance but he kept
falling down. 'Get up, boy!' shouted Mr Webster.
'We'll never get to the Manor House if you keep
falling over.'

4

'I can't help it,' said Jake, 'these brushes are very heavy. Can I put them on the cart?'

'What! And get soot all over my nice clean paintwork! Certainly not!' said Mr Webster.

'Mr Webster doesn't pay you to be cheeky,' said Slim. 'He pays you to clean chimneys, and do as you're told.'

'I don't pay him at all,' laughed Mr Webster. Slim laughed too. In fact he laughed so much, he nearly fell off the cart.

When they arrived at the Manor House, Jake was freezing. While Slim opened the gates, Jake put down the brushes for a moment, so he could blow on his hands and stamp his feet.

'What a fine house!' gasped Mr Webster. 'Look at all those beautiful chimneys to clean.'

Jake looked at the chimneys. They didn't seem beautiful to him. He was the one who would have to clean them.

Mr Webster drove the cart round to the back of the house and knocked at the kitchen door. A housemaid opened it. 'Come in at once,' she said kindly. 'You must be frozen. I'll get you all a bowl of nice hot broth.'

'That's very kind of you,' said Mr Webster. 'But just make it two bowls. The boy's not hungry. He couldn't even finish his breakfast.'

Jake looked longingly at the pot of steaming hot broth on the stove. So did Scruff.

'We'll start in the dining room first,' said Mr Webster, 'so if you'd be kind enough to run along and set the dust-sheet out, Jake, my boy, I'd be most obliged. Mr Slim and myself will be along to do the hard work when we've finished our broth.'

Jake had just finished putting the dust sheets out
when Mr Webster and Slim arrived. 'Haven't you
started yet?' snapped Mr Webster. 'Get up that
chimney, boy, before I get really angry.'

Jake hung his brush and scraper around his neck,
stepped into the fireplace and began to climb
up the wide chimney.

It was very dark inside the chimney and it took Jake a long time to reach the top. He began to brush away the thick soot that was caked on the chimney walls. 'I'm so tired I can hardly hold on,' he thought.

'Are you going to be up there all day?' Mr Webster's voice echoed up from the fireplace below. 'We've got another nineteen to do, so get a move on.'

'If only I could get away from them,' thought Jake. 'If only I could climb all the way up to the sky and never have to come down again.'

Jake had an idea. He could see daylight shining
down from the chimney pot. 'If I could get out on
to the roof, I could get away from them for an hour
or two,' he thought. 'I might be able to find
somewhere to hide and go to sleep. I'd get into
terrible trouble but it would be worth it.'

Jake climbed out on to the chimney stack and down to the roof. He could hear angry voices below.

'Perhaps I'd better go back,' he thought. 'They sound terribly fierce.' He looked out across the snow-covered fields and woods. 'No, I won't go back,' he decided. 'I've come this far. I might as well go on. But how am I going to get off the roof?'

Jake was good at climbing and he was not afraid of
heights but the snow had made the roof slippery.
As Jake worked his way round the chimney stack
he began to slide. He slithered down towards the
edge of the roof on a bed of snow. At the last
second he managed to grab hold of the corner of an
attic window as the snow crashed over the edge.

An angry cry came from below. 'He's on the roof!'
shouted Slim. Mr Webster just spluttered.
Jake took a deep breath and began to pull himself
up to the attic window. Luckily it was open.

'He's getting in through the window,' shouted Slim.
'Run up there and grab him!' shouted Mr Webster, from
underneath the pile of snow.

Jake fell into a small bedroom. 'I need to find
somewhere to hide,' he thought. He tiptoed to the
door and opened it. He found himself in a long
corridor with a staircase at either end of it.
Slim was running up one of the staircases so Jake
ran down the other. At the bottom of the stairs
there were lots of doors. Jake darted through
the first one. He was in a long room full of
pictures. Mr Webster was at the other end of the
room. He rushed towards Jake, knocking over
furniture as he did so. Jake turned and saw Slim
standing in the doorway. He was trapped. Slim leapt
forward to grab him but Jake dived between his legs.

14

Jake ran upstairs again. He had no idea where he was going. There were so many rooms, and corridors, and flights of stairs that he was soon completely lost. 'If I'm lost,' thought Jake, 'there's a good chance the others are too. Now all I've got to do is find somewhere to hide.'

Through an open door he could see a large, comfortable bed. 'I could hide under there,' he thought. He crept under the bed and waited nervously.

After a while Jake thought he heard someone come into the room. He closed his eyes tightly, expecting Mr Webster's huge hand to come under the bed and pull him out. Something cold and wet pressed against his cheek. 'Scruff!' gasped Jake. 'Where did you come from?'

Jake waited for ages but nobody came. He crept
from under the bed and looked around the room.

'All my life I've slept on piles of straw,' he
thought. 'I've always dreamed of sleeping in a clean
white bed like that. Even though I'm covered in soot
and I'm going to get into terrible trouble, I'm
going to risk it. Come on, Scruff, it's time for bed.'

Jake pulled back the covers and climbed in. Scruff
jumped on to the foot of the bed and curled up. They
were soon fast asleep.

A hand on Jake's shoulder shook him awake.

'Come on, Jake,' said his Mum. 'It's time for breakfast. I thought I told you not to let Scruff on your bed. I'm sure the people in the hotel would be very cross if they found out.'

On the way down to breakfast Jake told Mum about his dream. 'I can't think why I dreamt about sweeping chimneys,' he said.

'There's a picture of two chimney sweeps in the television room,' said Mum. 'That must have been what started it.'

'I don't remember that,' said Jake. 'I'll just nip in and have a look at it.'

'Hurry up, then,' said Mum. 'I'll see you in the breakfast room.'

Jake opened the door of the television room.

Webster & Co.~ Chimneysweeps
~ 1867 ~

ROOM

After breakfast Mum took Jake to the beach.

'Did you see the picture of the chimney sweeps?' she asked.

'Yes,' said Jake. 'I'm glad it's just a picture. I wouldn't like to meet those two in real life!'

Living in the past

Can you imagine what life would be like without gas or electricity? Not very many years ago the only way of keeping a house warm was to burn coal or wood in an open fireplace.

On a cold frosty morning the first job was to light the fire. First the cinders and ashes had to be cleared out of the grate. This was a dirty and messy job. Then the coal bucket had to be filled and the fire lit, using dry wood and coal. Rich people had fires in the kitchen, the sitting rooms, the dining room, and even the bedrooms. Poorer families lived and cooked in one room.

All the cooking was done on the fire or in an oven
next to the fire. You can imagine how dirty the pots
and pans got.

Coal makes everything sooty. Soot is dangerous
because it can burn. If chimneys are not swept
they catch fire. Then the house might burn down.

21

Some chimneys in old houses were so big that the only way of cleaning them was to climb up inside them and brush down the soot. This job was done by children.

Children also used to work down the mines where the coal came from. The miners worked in damp tunnels deep underground. They cut the coal with pickaxes. Then it was loaded onto little carts. The carts were pushed along the tunnels by children.

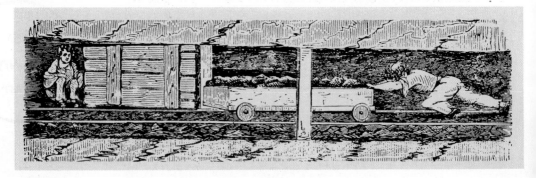

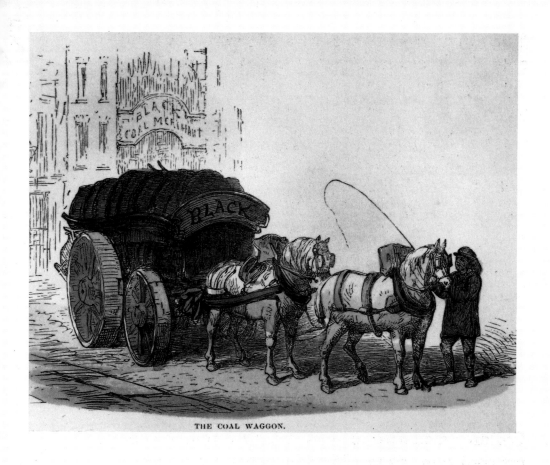

THE COAL WAGGON.

In the old days coal was delivered to people's
homes on carts pulled by horses. Horses had to be
fed and watered. They had to be brushed and combed
to keep them healthy and happy. Many of these jobs
were done by children too.

Today the law says that children must not work.
They must go to school instead. Would you like to
have lived in the old days?

Hans Andersen 1805–1875

This story was first told over a hundred years ago by Hans Andersen. Hans started life as a shoemaker but became one of the greatest storytellers of all time.
He lived in Denmark and wrote at a time when children were often treated unkindly. Only rich children went to school. Poor children had to work hard to earn money for their parents.

The little match girl

It was New Year's Eve. All over the city people were hurrying home to their warm houses. Everybody wanted to celebrate the end of the old year and the beginning of the new. 'Happy New Year!' they called to one another. Everywhere there was laughter.

It was snowing hard and it was beginning to get dark.
Along the street walked a little girl. She had no coat
and her thin dress was in tatters. She had no shoes,
and her feet were swollen from the cold.
The little girl held a bundle of matches in each of
her hands and she had more in her pocket. All that
day, she had not sold a single bundle.

Nobody took any notice of the little girl. Everybody wanted to get indoors out of the cold. They jostled past her on the pavement and would not stop to listen to what she was trying to say.

'Please will you buy my matches?' whispered the little girl. She could hardly get the words out because she was shivering so much.

Soon there were no more people crowding the streets. They were all safe behind their solid front doors. The little girl didn't know what to do. She sat down on a doorstep and began to cry.

How cold she was! If only she dare strike one of
her matches it might warm her a little bit.
The little girl took a match and struck it against
the wall of the house. The bright flame shone in
the darkness like a candle. For a moment everything
seemed to glow warm and bright. In her imagination
the little girl was wrapped in a warm dressing-gown,
and sitting in front of a glowing log fire.

  But in a moment the match burnt out. The little
girl was alone in the darkness on the cold stone
doorstep.

The little girl struck a second match. Its light glowed against the solid front door and the wreath of holly hanging above its brightly polished brass knocker. In her imagination she could see through the door and into the house itself. She saw a glittering Christmas tree decorated with shining glass balls and tiny candles. She saw a great table covered with the most delicious food; bowls of thick steaming soup, a goose stuffed with prunes and apples, plum puddings, and mince-pies. She saw children of her own age playing beneath the Christmas tree.

But then the second match burnt out and the vision was gone.

The little girl struck a third match. In its glow
she saw the gentle smiling face of her grandmother,
the only person who had ever loved her and been
kind to her. 'Grandmother!' gasped the little girl.
'I thought that you had left me forever. Please
stay with me.'

  The little girl was afraid that the beautiful
vision of her grandmother would disappear when her
match burnt out, just as the visions of the log fire
and the New Year's Eve feast had disappeared. With
trembling fingers she struck match after match after
match. The tiny flames seemed to glow with such a
strong bright light that the cold winter night
became like a bright summer's day. Grandmother
had never looked so young and beautiful. She
lifted the little girl gently in her arms and
together they flew to a happy place where there
was no cold, no tears, no hunger, and no fear.

On the morning of New Year's Day the people who
lived in the big house opened the door. On the
step was a small pile of burnt matches. They had
no idea where they had come from. They could know
nothing of the little match girl, nor of the
visions she had seen, nor of that happy land where
she and her grandmother had gone.

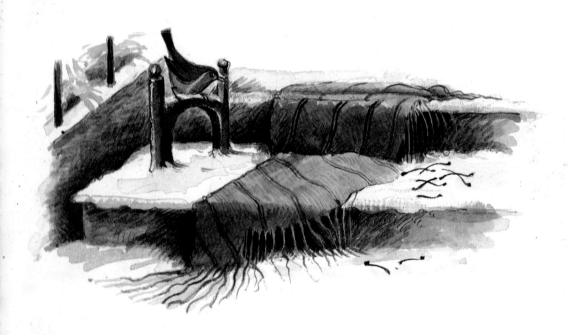